BOOK 5

THE MANUAL

SHOOTING/ROOTING/ BOOTING

CARL BEECH WITH
BAN HARDING
JACK THE LIFEGUARD

BIOGS

Carl	Ben	Jack

Carl is married to Karen and has two daughters. He's the leader of CVM (an international men's movement) and the founder of 'the code'. Previously a banker, church planter and senior pastor, he is convinced he is a great chef, plays the piano, loves cycling, movies and sci-fi books and caught a record-breaking catfish on the river Ebro in Spain.
Twitter @carlfbeech

Ben grew up in Devon, which opened up countless opportunities to work with mud, wheelbarrows, ice cream, cauliflowers, lime renders, boats and people. He used to think that following Jesus was what you did after you'd done all the fun bits of life and wanted to clean up your act before you croaked it. He gave his allegiance to Jesus when he was 20 and has never looked back. Ben is now a vicar.

Jack is an Intern at CVM as well as a part-time lifeguard. He has a passion for young people and helping people as a Street Pastor. Jack plans to get involved with local youth groups and prays that God can use his experiences to help others. He also enjoys watching the latest films, mountain biking and rugby.

Copyright © Carl Beech 2013
Published 2013 by CWR, Waverley Abbey House, Waverley Lane, Farnham, Surrey GU9 8EP, UK.
Registered Charity No. 294387. Registered Limited Company No. 1990308.
The right of Carl Beech, Ben Harding and Jack Undrell to be identified as the authors of this work has been asserted by them in accordance with the Copyright, Designs and Patents Act 1988.

For a list of National Distributors visit www.cwr.org.uk/distributors
Unless otherwise indicated, all Scripture references are from the Holy Bible: New International Version (NIV), copyright © 1973, 1978, 1984, 2011 by Biblica (formerly the International Bible Society). Other versions used: AV
Concept development, editing, design and production by CWR
Printed in Croatia by Zrinski
ISBN: 978-1-85345-941-2

Contents

BOOK 5

We've finally cracked it!
After being asked to write daily notes for men a number of times over the years, we've finally nailed it. So, in a nutshell, here you go and let the journey begin!

It's a simple and well-proven approach. The notes are between 200 and 300 words long. Each day begins with a verse and ends in a prayer. It will take you no more than a few minutes to read but I hope that what you read stays in your head throughout your day. The notes are numbered rather than dated, so it's OK if you miss a day to pick it back up. If you want to study with a group of guys you can easily keep track of where you are up to or swap ideas on that particular study online (we've a Facebook page). If you want to be part of a band of brothers internationally swapping thoughts, insights and prayer requests then you can do that as well by using our new Facebook page.

In each issue, I've asked some of my mates to contribute. In this one, big thanks to Ben Harding and Jack Undrell for their insights and thoughts. They're gunning for God and have some great things to say. We really hope that the subjects from Shooting to Booting speak into all our lives and help us stay on the narrow path.

So there it is. The Word of God has such power to inform and transform our lives, so let's knuckle down and get reading.

Your brother in Christ
Carl

[WHAT ARE WE SHOOTING FOR?]

01/ Blameless?

'Vindicate me, LORD, for I have led a blameless life ...' **Psalm 26:1a**

Now that's a prayer! My prayers go more like this: 'Vindicate me, Lord, for I'm really having a go at leading a blameless life but, to be honest, I need a bit of help right now ...'

I can't seem to help myself – wherever I go, I tend to get into some kind of trouble. The latest occasion was on a 'river rapids' ride with my kids. Having read the warning that one person in each boat would get absolutely drenched, I decided to put up my umbrella. (I am British, after all – and I was in the USA, so why spoil the stereotype?) Suffice to say that when I got off the ride, Wayne, the ride supervisor, was not a happy man! He pointed out the 'No umbrellas' sign and wandered off muttering something about 'stupid Brits ...'

Moderately harmless, really – but then there's stuff in my life and, I'm sure, in yours that's maybe a bit more toxic. Does that mean we can't call on

God for help, because in the shadows (or even in public) we're less than we should be? I don't think so. I think the aim of the game is to pursue holiness, but in the rough-and-tumble of life there will always be mishaps and misdemeanours. However, because we know Jesus we can call out to Him and find help in our time of need. Check out Hebrews 4:16!

Prayer: Thank You, Father, that You sent Jesus to die for me, even though I am far from blameless, and when I call out to You in the confusion of my up-and-down life, You hear my prayer. Amen.

02/ Trust me, I'm a banker

'I have trusted in the LORD and have not faltered.' **Psalm 26:1b**

Trust is a funny old thing. We all trust something or someone – a chair, that it won't give way; a doctor, that he knows what he's talking about; a plate of food, that it won't poison you. I'm a biker – I love motorbikes and have done ever since I was a kid – and sometimes, when I've been out riding at speed, I've looked at the tarmac slipping past underneath me and suddenly realised that I'm trusting no more than a hand's width of rubber tyre to keep me from a total wipeout.

In the last few years, our ability to trust has been damaged by several betrayals. Some have been instances of petty greed in public servants but some have been on an epic scale – even as I write this, a £1.4 billion bank trading fraud is being tried in court! Then there are the ongoing sex scandals as it emerges that much-loved TV personalities have preyed on young girls, and priests have abused children and the church has hushed it up.

So, who *can* we trust? Personally, I think we need to take the risk of giving people the benefit of the doubt and putting our trust in them, even though it lays us open to the risk of injury. That aside, though, we know from the Bible that God cannot lie (1 John 1:5) and we can persistently place our trust in Him. It seems to me that, when we do, that trust becomes an anchor that stops our lives drifting off-course – like, 'No matter what happens around me, no matter what I feel, I'll keep my head and my focus because I trust God.' I love the 'soft aggression' of this line in Psalm 26. It inspires me to persist in trusting Him, even when I feel bitterly disappointed by what I see around me.

Prayer: Help me to have an unwavering trust in You, Lord, that will truly be an anchor for my life. Amen.

03/Testing

'Test me, LORD, and try me,
examine my heart and my mind ...'
Psalm 26:2

A few years ago, I woke up with a start to find my heart thumping. It was a summer's morning, and it felt like it. Light was streaming in through the blinds and the air was warm. Somewhere in the distance, a pigeon was cooing – a sound I have associated with summer ever since I was a kid. So, why did I feel this mild panic? It took me a moment to figure it out. For some reason, I had put all these sensations together and thought I was due to sit an exam! I guess that, having had to sit them every summer at school and then on into my late twenties, I had come, somewhere in my subconscious, to associate that time of year with exams I wasn't always well prepared for.

I remember, after I finished my first degree at university, feeling totally awesome that I didn't ever have to do exams again - only to find out, when life took an unexpected turn and I pitched up at Bible college, that I did! And I expect there will be more exams at some stage (oh joy!). However, I think the Lord examines us in a different way. It's a kind of continual assessment (rather than a one- or two-hour crisis!) as each of us asks Him: 'How am I doing in Your eyes? What do You see in my heart that I need to sort out?'

Usually, the Holy Spirit has told us the answer to those questions before we even ask them. Let's be honest, though: it does take some guts to ask God to look closely at you! But do it and you'll reap the benefits. Slowly but surely, you'll find yourself becoming more of the man you know you ought to be, because you've given God access to your heart and mind.

Prayer: God, I give You full access to my heart and mind. Show me any stuff in the shadows of my life that I need to get sorted. Amen.

04/Faithful

'... for I have always been mindful of your unfailing love and have lived in reliance on your faithfulness.'
Psalm 26:3

Let's be frank about it: life isn't always a bunch of roses. Stuff happens, challenges crop up and things don't always pan out the way you thought they were going to – or ought to. One of the toughest lessons a parent has to learn, in the rollercoaster ride of bringing up kids, is that the little bundle of smiling, giggling humanity called a baby grows up to go through a stage called 'being a teenager'. Now, you may not have any kids yourself, or you may still be a teenager yourself, but bear with me. Most parents, when confronted with teenage stuff, or just kid stuff, soon realise that they need to correct their children from time to time if they want them to grow up to be half-decent human beings. It doesn't mean they don't love them when they tell 'em off. Usually, it's a sign that they do!

It's the same with God. We've fluffed up the stuff about love and forgotten that it also means that God will have to bring correction to our lives as well. So, yeah, God is loving and faithful, but I just don't think it's all about gooey feelings and hugs. After all, after He calls His Son 'beloved' and says He is 'well pleased' with Him, He sends Him into the desert for 40 days. Tough love! So, if God is putting *you* through the mill, now or at some future date, know that it's because He loves you. When the tough love happens, my advice is to suck it up and face up to it like a man, and ask the searching questions of yourself that make us all better blokes. Better still, surround yourself with good men who will give you their honest opinion of you along the way. To the wise, that's a priceless gift.

Prayer: Give me a fuller understanding of Your love and help me to accept Your discipline when it comes my way. Amen.

05/Watch your back

'I do not sit with the deceitful, nor
do I associate with hypocrites.'
Psalm 26:4

Someone once said that each of us is the average
of the five people we spend most time with. It's
an interesting thought. There's no doubt that the
people you associate with most have an impact
on your life. It's hard to hold the line when your
friendships take you to places and situations you
really don't want to be in. The thing is, the more
you open yourself up to that kind of compromise,
the more numbed and blunted your conscience
becomes.

I hate it when someone starts to tell me
something and then says that, if I want to hear
more, I have to promise not to tell anyone else.
In these situations, you have a choice: you can
either indulge them or tell them it's OK, they can
keep their information to themselves. It's such a
seductive thing – but actually I tend to think that
if someone is ready to tell me something they

shouldn't, I can probably never trust them with any confidences about my own life because it'd end up all over the place! I think this is very much connected with deceitfulness, because if you say you can keep a confidence but then pass it on to someone else, you're a liar.

Hypocrisy is another thing. I guess we can all be hypocrites at some time or another, but the habitually hypocritical have ugly characters. It's pretty grim, for instance, when people bleat on about morality but throw their weight around at home themselves or look at porn when they think no one's watching. Hang out with such people and it's going to affect you. So, watch the company you keep and, more important still, keep a grip on your own life!

Prayer: Keep me in good company. Alert me to those who would lead me to places I don't want to be in. Keep my motives pure and guard my tongue and my actions. Amen.

06/ Is that me?

'I abhor the assembly of evildoers
and refuse to sit with the wicked.'
Psalm 26:5

It's an interesting verse, this one. It would be easy
for me to wax lyrical about the wicked people all
around us and how we should avoid them like
the plague – but then I start to think: Perhaps I'm
one of them! What if someone was to look at the
totality of my life, in all its gory detail – how would
they describe me? Would they see me as an
'evildoer'? I think, in all honesty, the answer would
have to be yes.

Frankly, if it wasn't for the ongoing work of the
Holy Spirit in my life I would probably be a lost
cause. My life is like a building site, really. Some
of it is going up nicely and starting to look quite
presentable, maybe, but some of it is still just a
pile of rubble. So, yes, I try to watch who I keep
company with and I certainly feel that, as a man
of God, sometimes I need to stay away from

people who are obviously hell-bent on causing trouble.

But only, perhaps, to a degree. After all, if no one had bothered to cross the room and tell me about Jesus, I wouldn't be writing these devotionals now.

So, food for thought!

Prayer: Help me to keep an honest watch on my own life and to have a healthy sense, when I look at 'evildoers', of 'There but for the grace of God ...' Amen.

07/ Give it up for the Man

'I wash my hands in innocence,
and go about your altar, LORD,
proclaiming aloud your praise and
telling of all your wonderful deeds.'
Psalm 26:6-7

Sometimes when I'm in a church meeting I hang
my head in shame at the drivel we are singing. It
can all seem so me-centred, and often it sounds
more like something out of a Mills & Boon novel
than a shout-out to the Creator of the universe.
Contrast this with the Psalms, which can be very
emotional, yes, but almost invariably end up with
a declaration about how awesome God is. I think
we need to get back to that understanding of
worship. Us guys need to create more of a culture
of praise. I think we need to spend a bit more time
talking about the good things we see God doing
in our lives and the lives of other people around
us – that's obviously where praise starts. Not in a

soppy song but in a confident retelling of our own experience of His provision for us.

When my daughters were smaller, I used to tell them in the evenings about the stuff we saw God doing. Reading these verses today makes me think I need to get back to that – not just with my kids but in the general mix of daily life. If we make a habit of that kind of praise, I think it will spill over into our meetings on a Sunday (those of us who go to church, that is). So, make a start today. Find opportunities to speak up about the things God is doing around you. One thing is for sure, He likes it when we do that!

Prayer: Make me a man who proclaims Your praise and goes through life with a thankful attitude. Amen.

08/Nice pad

'LORD, I love the house where you live, the place where your glory dwells.' **Psalm 26:8**

I guess it's because of the presence of the Holy Spirit in our lives that we believe God is with us wherever we go. All through the Old Testament, His people longed for Him to be with them, but they had to be content with the Ark of the Covenant, the Tabernacle or the Temple.

I don't believe, though, that following Jesus was ever meant to be a solo journey – just me and Him. It's so important to meet up with other Christians. That's why in the Early Church they met each other daily and devoted themselves to teaching and prayer and so on (see Acts 2:42-47). In the strictest sense, perhaps, there is no longer a special place where the Lord 'dwells', but we should do our best to meet together somewhere to encounter Him. I say all this because I know that a lot of men have a love/hate relationship with the Church. It can be a struggle, after a long week, to drag yourself to yet another meeting. The thing is, though, that the Church is God's chosen vehicle to reach the world – and it does seem to be that when two or three gather together, there is a special sense of God's presence.

So, let's pray that He will give us a love for the Church. Not the building or the structure, I mean, but the people. Taking it a stage further, perhaps think about your practical commitment to the Church as well. How involved are you? Can you use your skills and talents, drive and grit to make a difference? If you feel that your own church is not the kind of place you could bring people to, ask yourself what you're going to do about it. Let's get ourselves to the place where we can truly say: 'Lord, I love being here on a Sunday, meeting with You and Your people!'

Prayer: Help me to love my church and show me what I can do to make it a place people really want to be in. Amen.

09/Blame game

'I lead a blameless life; deliver me
and be merciful to me.' **Psalm 26:11**

The words that leap out at me here are
'... be merciful to me.'

I was speaking at a meeting in London recently
where the talk was preceded by a meal. There
were a couple of hundred guys there, including
a load of men who weren't yet believers. This is
bread-and-butter stuff to me but just as I finished
eating I had a real sense that I needed to take
myself away and pray. Walking out of the room
into the main church, I found myself pacing up
and down the aisle, quietly praying that God
would help me. It was then that I noticed the
altar at the front. In my church tradition we don't
really do altars or anything, but I was really struck
by this one. As I started to walk towards it, I was
overcome by a sense of my own need for God.

The nearer I got to the altar, the smaller I seemed
to feel. It was when I arrived right at the front of

the church that I asked God to be merciful to me, a sinful man. It wasn't anything dramatic, and it didn't give me a warm, fuzzy feeling or anything. It was just a straightforward prayer in response to my own sense of needing God's grace.

I think that often, as men, we rely heavily on our own ability to get a job done and so sometimes it's crucial to bring ourselves back to reality and spend some time at the foot of the cross. Have a think about this today. Perhaps take a walk at lunchtime and pop into a church and sit down and reflect on God's amazing grace and utter the words: 'Thank You for Your mercy to me ...'

Prayer: Thank You, Father, for Your grace and mercy. Thank You for Jesus. Thank You that even though I am a sinful man You reached out to me. Amen.

10/Spirit level

'My feet stand on level ground; in the great congregation I will praise the LORD.' **Psalm 26:12**

Jesus told us to build our house on the rock (check out Matt. 7:24-27). Here, the psalmist reminds us to keep our feet on level ground. Why do we need to keep getting these prompts? Because it's so easy to find ourselves on ground that is unstable or uneven, that will let us down or trip us up.

So, how do we get our feet on level ground? I think it's simply about putting our trust and confidence in God and keeping close to Him when we make decisions or take action. I think it's also about surrounding ourselves with good and wise people. Just recently, my wife Karen and I had to make a pretty crucial decision about something to do with our life and work. I could see so many ways forward, but was feeling a bit muddled by it all. That's rare for me, but I knew that in order to do what would please God and keep us on level ground we needed someone else to pray with us. So, in the words of a certain TV quiz, I phoned a friend.

He came round and prayed with us through the decision we had to make. The clarity that came to us then, by talking things through in that prayerful way, was astonishing. Us blokes tend to think we are all-capable and all-sufficient. Let me tell you, that is a sure way to lose your balance and fall down.

Prayer: Surround me with good people and save me from being so proud that I don't think I need wise input from others. Keep me on level ground, Father, and protect me from losing my balance and making stupid decisions. Amen.

[BODYBUILDING]

11/Crack on!

'Therefore encourage one another and build each other up, just as in fact you are doing.' **1 Thessalonians 5:11**

When I ran the London Marathon a couple of years ago, I decided to put my name on the front of my T-shirt. It was the best move I ever made – I reckon that simple trick took about 10 miles off the race for me. Why? Because all the way round the course people were cheering me on like crazy. On every corner, every straight, every hill and every flat there were crowds of people applauding the runners and cheering them on by name. I couldn't believe the difference this encouragement made to me – and this was from complete strangers!

The problem with us blokes is that we can be really slow to dish out the praise. We get our heads down and all too easily take people for granted. The thing is, though, that when we do take time to encourage those around us and build them up, it can have an amazing effect. It's true, too, that we reap what we sow. If we make the effort to cheer on those around us, it will probably come back in our direction as well.

So, don't just think about this one, crack on and do it! Find cause and opportunity today to encourage other people. Do what you can to bring out the best in those around you. Look for the good and tell them what you see. Even a 'That's amazing what you did there ...' can go a long way.

Prayer: I commit myself today to make sure that the words that leave my mouth are more often encouraging and building up than critical and tearing down. Amen.

12/ Be secure

'And by him we cry, '*Abba*, Father.'
The Spirit himself testifies with our
spirit that we are God's children.'
Romans 8:15-16

So, what's this got to do with cheering people
on? Everything, I reckon. Let me explain. I think
that a lot of the time the reason us blokes don't
encourage other people is because we are
envious or insecure and the last thing we want
is for someone else to look better than us or
excel more than us in any way. How sad is that?
If anything, as followers of Jesus we *should* be
rooting for other people to be better than us and
hoping beyond all hope that the next generation
in particular achieves far more than we ever have.

We need to find our identity and security in the
fact that God is our Father, not in the hope that
other people will see us as the next big shot. If
I'm anxious that not everyone will see me as the
'big man', if I feel threatened if there's a bigger
gorilla in the room than me, that's a sure route

to becoming the kind of man who postures, positions himself and throws his weight around. And that's not a pretty sight.

So, let's focus on who we are in Christ and not on who we might be in other people's eyes. That's a massive distraction that can lead us to ugly places we really don't want to go to.

Prayer: Help me to see myself as You see me and not to be anxious about how anyone else sees me. Help me to keep in mind that I am performing to an audience of one! Amen.

13/Band of brothers

'Honour all men. Love the brotherhood. Fear God. Honour the king.' **1 Peter 2:17 (AV)**

Let's think about what it means to honour all men and love the brotherhood. How does that work out in practice, I wonder? I love the *Band of Brothers* stuff - the story of an infantry platoon in the Second World War that went through training together and then fought their way through Western Europe all the way to Hitler's mountain lair, the Eagle's Nest. It's a fascinating story in itself, but what grips most men is the way those guys were prepared to spill their own blood for each other and those who survived remained lifelong friends. Perhaps it was because they went through hell together.

Men bond in adversity, that much is true. However, those of us who haven't fought in a war and haven't had to spill their blood for one another may need a different motivation and method. How about a revival of that good old-time thing called 'honour'? You know the kind of thing: not speaking ill of someone behind their back. Going the extra mile to be there for someone when it's all going pear-shaped for them. Not stabbing a bloke in the back at work in a situation where it's either him or you. These are normal kinds of things but they're often neglected nowadays.

I don't quite know how to capture this thought succinctly except to say: Let's be blokes who are there for each other. Dependable, not flaky, and ready to go the distance in friendship. This applies no matter what age the other guy is or what his status, wealth or profession seems to be. The only caveat to that is that I reckon older men have earned the right to be listened to a bit more than the rest of us. We're rubbish at honouring their generation, so maybe we should start with them.

Prayer: Make me a man of honour who is there for other men, through thick and thin. Amen.

---

¹⁴/Deal with it!

'If your brother or sister sins, go and point out their fault, just between the two of you. If they listen to you, you have won them over.'
Matthew 18:15

This passage (which is worth a read-through later) goes on to talk through the whole process of how to deal with conflict in the church. So many guys fall at the first hurdle, though. I have an expression at CVM: 'Let's keep the floor clean and sweep up any dirt quickly!' So often, in teams or among friends, little things can get on our nerves – and can soon become very big things if they're not dealt with promptly. I've so often seen a serious, long-term breakdown in relationships happen in this way.

So, what's the answer? An honest chat over a beer, I reckon. It doesn't have to be confrontational at all, if we approach things as mates. Here's an example. A member of my team came over to me the other day and said something like: 'You seem to be juggling too much these days. Are you getting enough downtime?' This then progressed to: 'It's just that I can see you're not getting enough time to listen to people – including me ...' That was the gist of it, anyway. It was great! It led to some good conversations, and some good decisions were made – and in future I'll keep an eye on how attentive I'm being to my team, won't I?

Of course, there may be really difficult conversations as well sometimes; but if you work on creating a culture of trust, openness and mateship it does become somewhat easier! So, let's all man up and bite the bullet when we need to. Just be gracious and gentle. Oh, and one final thing: remember to be gracious and gentle when you're on the receiving end, too!

Prayer: Keep my friendships real, honest and open. Give me the guts to speak out when I need to, and the grace to receive a word of advice when it's needed as well. Amen.

15/Keep your door open

'Share with the Lord's people who are in need. Practise hospitality.'
Romans 12:13

Let's focus on the last part of this verse. Hospitality is a funny thing – it comes completely naturally to some people, but for others it's a real struggle because, in all honesty, when their work is done for the day they'd rather go below deck and batten down the hatches! I tend to be like that myself. I can become a real recluse on holidays, or when I get some downtime. I'm a weird mix of introvert and extrovert, but I definitely get my strength from being on my own or just with my family!

The thing is, though, that there is a remarkable blessing that comes from opening your home to other people. Over the years, Karen and I have played host to people from overseas (who are totally non-Western in their approach to things) as well as, for a whole year, a gap-year youth worker who had access to nearly every area of our lives! All I can say is that I have been left all the richer for it, whatever the ups and downs. So, come on, fella, how about it? What about opening your home up at Christmas to someone who would otherwise be alone? What about making sure that every month you have a meal with someone that you host? After all, 'Practise hospitality' is a command, not a suggestion!

I guarantee you that, at the end of your days, one thing is for sure: you'll be grateful for the many people you've shared your life with.

Prayer: Show me where I can be more generous with my time and more hospitable. Bring people and situations into my life that will challenge me to open my home and my heart to others. Amen.

[BOOT CAMP!]

16/Take it on the chin

'Know then in your heart that as a man disciplines his son, so the LORD your God disciplines you.'
Deuteronomy 8:5

As a dad, I soon came to realise that if I gave my kids everything they asked for, I would ruin them. I also came to realise very early on that if I wanted them to grow up into decent human beings, I needed to set them some boundaries and enforce them. It was all part of loving them and not rejecting them. That's the weird thing, you see: the more permissive you are as a dad, the more 'do-as-you-please', the more your kids will ultimately feel rejected rather than loved and blessed.

Here's the rub, though: God treats us just the same. He cares far too much about us not to bring us under discipline when we need it. And let's face it, I would much rather learn lessons now and get my character sorted out than take a massive hit at the end of my days when I finally come into the presence of Jesus and He looks me in the eye with an air of disappointment!

So, if you're serious about walking with God, get serious about the fact He may want to deal with stuff in your life as part of His 'refining' process. My advice when those times come? Take it on the chin like a man – in fact, suck it up! Learn the lessons, resolve to be different, dust yourself down and then crack on!

Prayer: Help me to accept the discipline of the Lord and become the man I know I ought to be. Amen.

17/Race fit

'Do you not know that in a race all the runners run, but only one gets the prize? Run in such a way as to get the prize.' **1 Corinthians 9:24**

When I cycled from Land's End to John o'Groats, I had to get fit for it. The next year, when I cycled from Calais to Nice via the Alps, I had to get fitter. It was the same story when I cycled from Nice to Naples – I couldn't just get on a bike and do it, I had to do the hard work and get myself race fit. That meant long runs and rides and hours on an indoor trainer, watching my diet and giving up lazy habits.

The parallels with the Christian life are amazing. The Bible makes it clear that we are in the race of our lives – there's no place for couch-potato Christianity or half-hearted 'power walking'. So, what does running in such a way as to get the prize look like? Well, for me I think it means taking the call of the gospel seriously and placing it first above everything else. It means not only taking every opportunity to make Jesus known but also being seen by others as one of the most generous people they know. It means being really serious about knowing God and talking to Him in prayer. Does that sound hardcore? Too right. Following Jesus is not a jog in the park, it's a marathon that requires us to push ourselves hard until the race is finally over.

Let's face it, the athletes who win gold medals do so because they train harder than everyone else. The glory they attain on the podium is the result of months, if not years, of full-on training. Worth thinking about.

Prayer: I commit to train hard, work hard and pursue God with all my heart, soul, mind and strength. Amen.

18/Focus

'No one serving as a soldier gets entangled in civilian affairs, but rather tries to please his commanding officer. Similarly, anyone who competes as an athlete does not receive the victor's crown except by competing according to the rules.' **2 Timothy 2:4-5**

Does this mean we shouldn't be concerned at all about the stuff that's going on in the world? Of course not. It's more about getting distracted from the main event: the fight of our lives to make Jesus known. So, what are 'civilian affairs'? Perhaps it's chasing down that promotion? When it occupies all your thoughts, that's a civilian affair taking precedence over the gospel. Or what about pursuing that bigger house at the expense of giving appropriately to the Lord's work?

Two great contrasts in Luke are the rich man who couldn't give up his wealth (18:18-30) and Zacchaeus (19:1-10), who in the end wanted to give his possessions away. The former was entangled in civilian affairs; the latter set his heart on Jesus and His kingdom. I guess it could also apply to stuff like being fixated on our image or fitness. Life is about staying balanced, but within that balance our priority should be Jesus and what He wants. So, have a think about the stuff that's going on around you and the distractions that are consuming your energy, time and money. Perhaps you should cut them out if they feel like they're taking you further away from your first love, Jesus.

Now, hear me correctly in all of this. I'm not, of course, calling us all to some puritanical life of misery – far from it. I'm simply saying: If you notice that some things in life are getting an unhealthy grip on you, do something about it and do it quickly. Get some balance back into things and keep the main thing the main thing!

Prayer: Help me to keep my eyes fixed on Jesus, the Pioneer and Perfecter of my faith. Keep me alert to distractions and wise about the things I put my resources into. Amen.

19/Testing

'Examine yourselves to see whether you are in the faith; test yourselves. Do you not realise that Christ Jesus is in you – unless, of course, you fail the test?'

2 Corinthians 13:5

Let me start by saying that I have full assurance that I am in Christ and that He is in me. However, I do regularly spend time making sure that I'm on track and that the essentials of what we believe as followers of Jesus are firmly rooted in my heart and mind. The thing is, so often discipleship becomes more about our lifestyle and how to be blessed – in effect, a kind of life coaching – than about the core of the gospel message. Which means we can go for long periods of time without really remembering what it's all about when everything else is stripped away: that Jesus came to save us. I once went to a church for over a year and didn't once hear a statement of the gospel. They were good people and faithful to the Bible, but they had taken the message for granted.

I look at a verse like this and it makes me ponder a few things. I remember my conversion and the process that led up to it, my discovery of Jesus and the sheer, overwhelming power of the revelation that God is real. I think back to the day I first realised that a man had died in my place. I recall the times when I have known God's grace and the times when I have known His forgiveness and mercy. I examine myself, and I ask the question: Am I still walking with Jesus in the way I should? Does my life now reflect the revelation of Jesus I had when I was 18? It's a good process to go through, I think.

Prayer: As I think about my first encounter with You, or the process I went through before I truly understood what You have done for me, I commit again to walk with You, with all my heart, soul, mind and strength. Amen.

20/Thorns

'The seed falling among the thorns refers to someone who hears the word, but the worries of this life and the deceitfulness of wealth choke the word, making it unfruitful.'
Matthew 13:22

What are you shooting for? What is it you're chasing? Over the years, I've had the privilege of knowing some amazing people – bright, capable, skilled in loads of areas, good with people and so on. Every one I am thinking of was also passionately pursuing the kingdom and gunning for people to meet with Jesus. More than a few times, I felt sure they were likely to end up 'in the bush' somewhere, telling remote tribes about Jesus! Or else I was pretty sure they would end up being leading lights in a local church. Then, in every case, something happened. They started to take their eyes off the ball and focus on more worldly prizes. They started to accumulate wealth, 'build bigger barns', go on epic holidays and worry more about the size of their en-suite bathrooms than whether they were seeing the kingdom of God at hand. Absolutely tragic! All that potential starved and choked by material possessions and stuff that is, essentially, nothing but smoke and mirrors.

I don't have a problem with people having nice houses, cars and holidays, but I get wound up when I see the pursuit of such things taking people away from their first love. It's such a tragic waste – a direct result of seduction. Jesus saw it coming, and down the centuries others have repeated His warnings against it – but it still happens. So, ask the question, fella: What are you shooting for and what is it you're truly pursuing?

Prayer: Father, help me to stay focused on what really matters, and alert my conscience when I start to take my eyes off the ball. Amen.

[SIGNS & WONDERS]

21/Rainbow warrior

'... there before me was a throne in heaven with someone sitting on it. And the one who sat there had the appearance of jasper and ruby. A rainbow that shone like an emerald encircled the throne. Surrounding the throne were twenty-four other thrones, and seated on them were twenty-four elders. They were dressed in white and had crowns of gold on their heads. From the throne came flashes of lightning, rumblings and peals of thunder.'
Revelation 4:2-5

I was driving through the countryside the other day. The sky was filthy dark, but blazing across it was the most stunning rainbow I think I have ever seen. It was like a massive arc of power surging from one point on the horizon to another.

No wonder people say there is treasure at the end of a rainbow – there is! But the real treasure is not a stash of gold coins left behind by some cheeky leprechaun, but a golden promise – the blazing promise of salvation.

As a rainbow arcs across the sky, so the image of the rainbow arcs through the Bible. We see it first in Genesis, get a single glimpse of it in Ezekiel and finally encounter it again in Revelation. The symbol of God's promise never again to abandon His creation to total destruction wraps the start and finish of our story.

Next time you see the rainbow, remember the promise of salvation the Lord has made and never broken. If you are His son, He has sworn to be for you, to be your Rock and your Defender. He will not let your foot slip.

Prayer: Thank You, Lord, that You use creation to tell Your story of rescue and protection. May I be a rainbow warrior, saved by Your promise and serving Your kingdom. Amen.

22/Data protection

'The seventy-two returned with joy and said, "Lord, even the demons submit to us in your name." He replied, "I saw Satan fall like lightning from heaven. I have given you authority to trample on snakes and scorpions and to overcome all the power of the enemy; nothing will harm you. However, do not rejoice that the spirits submit to you, but rejoice that your names are written in heaven."' **Luke 10:17-20**

Picture the scene as Jesus' apprentices return from a successful mission. They were sent out like lambs among wolves and are stoked to have found that actually they are the ones with the teeth! They have been smashing through some of the stuff that had poisoned the communities they went to – sickness, trauma and uncontrollable spiritual interference.

Jesus rejoices that humankind's old enemy has begun to get beaten, but for His apprentices there is something more important than glorious victory. He reminds them that what really counts is not what they do in God's name but the fact that their own names are known to God and 'written in heaven'. That is what gives them their identity and status.

Let's not fall into the trap of doing stuff *for* God while forgetting who we are *in* God. Serving the King feels different when you know you are His son. Our service has to come from our identity – the other way round is a bottomless pit of insecurity and striving.

Prayer: Lord, thank You that You care more about who I am than what I do. Show me what it means that my name is written in heaven, so that I can live like Your son, not Your slave. Amen.

23/The Master's voice

'My sheep listen to my voice; I know them, and they follow me. I give them eternal life, and they shall never perish; no one will snatch them out of my hand. My Father, who has given them to me, is greater than all; no one can snatch them out of my Father's hand.'
John 10:27-30

Whenever I turn on my car stereo, it displays the message: NO CODE. It works OK, plays music and stuff; but anyone could nick it and use it because it hasn't been security-protected. It hasn't been linked to me personally by a code I have given it, so it could belong to anyone.

Jesus makes it very clear that, as He is the Good Shepherd, His sheep cannot be stolen, from Him. There will be no rustling and no hustling. They belong to Him and they are safe, security-protected.

Who are Jesus' sheep? Ordinary people who recognise, listen to and follow His voice: the code that identifies and protects His property. When Brazil won the World Cup in 2002, its star player Kaká stripped off his yellow shirt to reveal a T-shirt that said simply: 'I belong to Jesus.' How could he say that so confidently? Because he recognises, listens to and follows his Master's voice.

How do we hear the Master's voice? Here are a couple of starters:
- Crack open your Bible and ask: 'Lord, speak to me through Your Word.'
- Listen when you pray – it's a two-way thing. Remember, only a rabble babbles! Give Him space to answer your prayer. Usually, He is more eager to speak than we are to listen.

And next time you type your PIN, smile to yourself and give thanks that you belong to Jesus!

Prayer: Lord, thank You that You have chosen me and identified me as Your own. May I amplify You and transmit Your message of hope, security, invitation and identity. Amen.

24/ Breakfast of champions

'Jesus said to them, "Very truly I tell you, it is not Moses who has given you the bread from heaven, but it is my Father who gives you the true bread from heaven. For the bread of God is the bread that comes down from heaven and gives life to the world." "Sir," they said, "always give us this bread." Then Jesus declared, "I am the bread of life. Whoever comes to me will never go hungry, and whoever believes in me will never be thirsty."' **John 6:32-35**

If you were some food, what would you be? A fry-up - not complicated but hearty and a bit lardy? Or how about a curry: well-travelled, adaptable but a bit feisty? Or maybe caviar with champagne: refined, subtle and rich, but an acquired taste?

It's interesting that Jesus describes Himself as bread. He is such a genius with images! Bread is not just for special occasions but for every day. It is – or should be – available to all, rich and poor. It is not only nourishing but satisfying. It is for eating: not for looking at and admiring from a distance but for filling yourself up with. And it needs to be broken before it can be eaten ...

Jesus is the Living Bread, who invites us to feed on Him, to get nourished and fuelled up by Him – and then show others where the good eating is!

As one bloke described evangelism, it's just 'one beggar showing another beggar where to get bread'. Tuck in, lad!

Prayer: Lord, thank You that You want me to be nourished and satisfied. Help me to get my fill of You. Give me this day my daily bread! Amen.

[TOUGH VERSES]

25/ Who's the big man?

'At that time the disciples came to Jesus and asked, "Who, then, is the greatest in the kingdom of heaven?" He called a little child to him, and placed the child among them. And he said: "Truly I tell you, unless you change and become like little children, you will never enter the kingdom of heaven."' **Matthew 18:1-3**

It's well known that I'm not really into children's action songs in church. I'm not a 'fuzzy-wuzzy bear' or an 'iggly-wiggly worm', I'm a man! I hate it when the kids' workers tell us to do the actions and then make us do 'em again because we weren't doing it enough the first time. It makes me want to start a Gangnam-stylie dance out the exit door.

But Jesus isn't asking us to be childish, He's asking us to become like children. For me, that means being full of optimism, joy and faith. I look at the way kids believe in things and put their trust in them so quickly and I compare that to my own cynicism and I totally get what Jesus is saying. I feel the same when I hear younger people talk about their hopes and dreams for the future. Some might say they're being naive, but I think: 'You go for it – and don't look back!'

Life can be bruising, for sure, and the enemy likes to use the bad to damage our belief in other people and the possibility of a better future. So, how do we keep our heads and hearts full of hope? I think we can do it by doing hopeful, faith-filled things. Start to take risks again. Put your trust in an idea or a person even if it makes you nervous. And do it again, even if things go wrong. That's what it means, I believe, to be like a little child.

Prayer: Fill me with optimism.
Help me to resist cynicism.
Give me a childlike faith
that is full of trust. Amen.

26/Watch it!

'If anyone causes one of these little ones – those who believe in me – to stumble, it would be better for them to have a large millstone hung round their neck and to be drowned in the depths of the sea.'
Matthew 18:6

To get to the point, this verse is not, as it's often supposed to be, concerned with child abuse. It's talking about preaching and teaching that lead believers in Jesus – and particularly new ones – astray. There's an awful lot of rubbish teaching out there. 2 Timothy 4:3 calls it stuff that our ears are itching to hear. It's stuff that makes us feel good or gets us chasing after things that aren't exactly Jesus-centred. You know the kind of thing I mean: If you give this much money, or pray this type of prayer, you'll end up with a new white Mercedes (or maybe just a shiny new iPad, if your tastes are more modest). It's life coaching instead of the gospel and consumerism instead of giving your possessions away, greed

instead of generosity and individualism instead
of community.

I've got to be frank with you, this stuff makes me
feel sick to the stomach. If you're getting a load
of teaching that speaks to your needs, wants and
desires but neglects the demands of the gospel,
your alarm bells should be ringing. Sure, God
wants the very best for us and wants to bless us;
but if you are being fed mostly with stuff that is all
about you rather than Jesus, you should be very
concerned. There is a frightening warning here
to preachers who point people away from Jesus.
Let's keep our focus on Him!

**Prayer: Help me to stay alert
for false teaching that points
me away from You. Amen.**

27/Surgery

'If your hand or your foot causes you to stumble, cut it off and throw it away. It is better for you to enter life maimed or crippled than to have two hands or two feet and be thrown into eternal fire.' **Matthew 18:8**

What we are talking about here is radical, brutal surgery in order to resist temptations that could lead you to places you really don't want to go to.

When I was in Amsterdam with a colleague recently, we went for a walk to a part of the city where he used to go to church 30 years ago. For him, it was a bit of a walk down memory lane; for me, it was a startling illustration of the enemy's snares. I hadn't realised that his church had been in the heart of the red-light district! Walking past window after window in which women stood practically naked, offering sex to anyone who would pay for it, was both depressing and a wake-up call at the same time. Every time I saw a man walking in and the curtain being drawn, I could almost hear the enemy laughing. I could also imagine the pain there must be in the lives of the women behind the glass. It was heartbreaking. The wake-up call for me was simply a strong sense of the truth of something we often say: 'There but for the grace of God ...' These were ordinary men and women whose lives had taken a toxic path. I was grateful that the Lord had steered me onto the narrow way.

I'm trying to keep these 'tough verse' devotions brief and to the point, so let me just say this: Take action, mate! If you have an area of weakness in your life, do whatever it takes to win that battle – even if it comes at a cost. Fight hard and fight tough. None of us wants to give the enemy a laugh, or to help to destroy someone else's life.

Prayer: Keep me alert to the enemy's plan to destroy lives – including mine. Amen.

28/Rescue squad

'If a man owns a hundred sheep, and one of them wanders away, will he not leave the ninety-nine on the hills and go to look for the one that wandered off? And if he finds it, truly I tell you, he is happier about that one sheep than about the ninety-nine that did not wander off. In the same way your Father in heaven is not willing that any of these little ones should perish.'
Matthew 18:12-14

I remember a terrible moment when one of my daughters was really small and she went missing for all of five minutes at church. It turned out she was with one of my friends, but it frightened the life out of me! It also showed me just how much I loved my kids. God feels the same for us and more. After all, He loves us so much that He sent His Son to die on a cross and He watched it happen, refusing to intervene, because He was determined to make a way for us to be with Him.

My prayer is that I would develop the same heart, not only to introduce new people to Jesus but to bring back to Him those who once used to walk with Him. I wonder how good we are at keeping in touch with those who kind of drift away to the margins of the church. One thing's for sure, according to these verses we should be really concerned about people who have a faith in Jesus but start to lose it. I guess it would be even better if we developed such a sense of dynamic community that people were much less likely to drift away. So, let's try to tackle the issue these verses point to. Let's work hard at mateship and put effort into the life of the Church.

Prayer: Give me Your heart to see people stick close to You and to go after those who are drifting away. Give me Your heart for the life of the Church. Amen.

29/Grit your teeth

'Then Peter came to Jesus and asked, "Lord, how many times shall I forgive my brother or sister who sins against me? Up to seven times?" Jesus answered, "I tell you, not seven times, but seventy-seven times." **Matthew 18:21-22**

What this does not mean is that you have to forgive someone 77 times, keeping an accurate count and detailed record of each occasion, and then tell them where to go when they commit offence number 78. That's called 'religion' and it's the kind of thing the Pharisees might have done. What Jesus tends to do when dishing out this kind of teaching is speak to our hearts. He isn't setting a standard or a target, He's telling us that no matter what the situation is, we must keep forgiving. The thing is, as someone once said, not forgiving someone and remaining bitter is like giving them space in your head rent-free. In other words, not only is forgiving the right thing to do –

because, after all, Jesus forgives us – it's the way to restore peace to your own life.

There have been more than a few occasions when I have been hurt by things people have said or done. Everything in me wanted to defend myself, to put the record straight – and wallow in some angst. On a couple of occasions, I've written amazing emails (that I haven't sent) in the hope that expressing my clearly righteous anger (ahem!) would make me feel better. Let me tell you something: it never works. Jesus knows this and that's why He tells us to forgive.

A brilliant book on this is R.T. Kendall's *Total Forgiveness* – if you're struggling with this kind of stuff in any way, it's a cracking read. For now, though, I suggest that if you feel any lingering bitterness you take a moment to put your head straight and steel yourself to say this prayer.

Prayer: Where I need to sort something out, no matter how painful it is or how wound up I am about it, please give me the backbone and the grit to deal with it and forgive. Amen.

[DIVIDED WE FALL]

30/United we stand

'I appeal to you, brothers and sisters, in the name of our Lord Jesus Christ, that all of you agree with one another in what you say and that there be no divisions among you, but that you be perfectly united in mind and thought.'
1 Corinthians 1:10

As we'll see in the next reading, there was a spot of bother brewing in the Corinthian church. Basically, the believers were far from having the same mind and were splitting up into factions all over the shop. When teams start to do that, they fall apart, whether it's on the playing field or in the workplace or the church. If disunity isn't dealt with swiftly, it can take the whole ship down very quickly. It could be a dispute over the vision and direction of the organisation. It could be an issue of leadership which divides people into different camps. It could be a row over strategy or perhaps just a good, old-fashioned personality clash.

These things happen, of course, but what we need are good ways to deal with them. So often pride gets in the way. People dig their heels in and refuse to budge – and in the end it's the whole darn show that budges as it all falls apart. Basically, we need to get over ourselves!

Other causes may be more principled. You may genuinely think that something that's going on strikes at the heart of something you believe in passionately. In such cases, I think, if no one is hearing your point of view it is often best to take yourself quietly out of the picture. I know some people who have hung around in churches in such situations and basically done their best – perhaps without meaning to – to destabilise the whole thing. That's not a good way forward. So, in a nutshell: pursue peace – and, if necessary, do so by removing yourself.

Prayer: Help me to be a man who unites rather than divides, a team man and not a man who pursues his own interests, driven by pride. Amen.

31/Follow my leader

'What I mean is this: one of you says, "I follow Paul"; another, "I follow Apollos"; another, "I follow Cephas"; still another, "I follow Christ." Is Christ divided? Was Paul crucified for you? Were you baptised in the name of Paul?' **1 Corinthians 1:12-13**

This is what lay behind at least part of the row that was ripping the church in Corinth apart. Presumably, it was all about who was the best speaker or teacher, who was the wisest or most charismatic – with a sprinkling of purists who were all for Jesus and Him alone! Paul is totally hacked off with the lot of them. He even goes on to say he's glad he didn't baptise any of 'em, in case they put *him* before Jesus!

And that's the deal here. Jesus comes first before everything and everyone, including our leaders. That's not to say that we shouldn't have leaders, but we should avoid the trap of dividing into different camps. Personally, I think team leadership works best. That way, you get a mix of insights and abilities that (hopefully) complement each other. The thing to do then is recognise each leader's strengths and not favour one above another. (I'm talking about church stuff here, but I think this holds true across the board.)

It's important to remember when we read about the way everything went pear-shaped in Corinth that we are basically witnessing the problems of having lots of immature believers in one place. These sorts of rows shouldn't blow up where there are seasoned followers of Jesus. That's worth noting for future reference.

So, be sure to honour your leaders – but also to put Jesus first. And be sure to be wise and mature in how you deal with situations where a leader maybe gets up your nose and you're tempted to speak out against them or jump ship to another church whose leader seems more dynamic. This can really set back God's mission.

Prayer: Help me to avoid the immature trap of having a favourite leader and ending up in their camp. Amen.

32/Fool

'Where is the wise person? Where is the teacher of the law? Where is the philosopher of this age? Has not God made foolish the wisdom of the world?' **1 Corinthians 1:20**

Here are some famous(ish) quotes by famous philosophers. I thought it would be good for us all to get some intellectual stimulation from these notes for a change...

'What we have to learn to do, we learn by doing' – Aristotle in *Nicomachean Ethics*

'I think, therefore I am' – René Descartes in *Discourse on the Method*

'Laughter is an affection arising from the sudden transformation of a strained expectation into nothing' – Immanuel Kant in *Critique of Judgement*

'Every man, wherever he goes, is encompassed by a cloud of comforting convictions, which move with him like flies on a summer day' – Bertrand Russell in 'Dreams and Facts', in *Sceptical Essays*

Interesting? How about this one? 'I can't get no satisfaction' – Mick Jagger

Or how about this, from Frank Sinatra?
'Dobedobedo ...'

And that, for me, is the bottom line in all of this.
Philosophy can be hugely important in shaping
our understanding of the world and our lives – I
wouldn't want to pour scorn on it at all – but in
the final analysis, as Paul says in 1 Corinthians
1:22-23, 'Jews demand signs and Greeks look for
wisdom, but we preach Christ crucified ...' That
kind of cuts through it all for me. Jesus said some
truly profound things: Repent and believe, forgive
one another, love your neighbour as yourself,
love your enemies, give to the poor – you can
take your pick from any number of hugely
countercultural statements that still challenge
us today. When all is said and all is done, look
to Jesus and you'll find that His teachings make
much better sense of the world than any of the
world's greatest philosophers.

**Prayer: Give me a simple,
uncluttered faith, which
centres on the fact that Jesus
loves me. Help me to absorb
more deeply His hugely
radical teachings. Amen.**

33/No excuses

'And so it was with me, brothers and sisters. When I came to you, I did not come with eloquence or human wisdom as I proclaimed to you the testimony about God. ... I came to you in weakness with great fear and trembling.' **1 Corinthians 2:1,3**

People think that because I do a lot of public speaking, I must be an extrovert; but nothing could be further from the truth. I don't like doing door-to-door evangelism and I'm fairly useless at small talk. I didn't go to a private school or a top university, and I'm a pretty average man. However, none of that is any excuse when it comes to sharing the gospel.

For me, this has been one of the most startling discoveries about telling people about Jesus. Sure, they will sometimes get a bit hot under the collar – but generally I have found that people are fascinated to hear about my faith. Paul goes on to imply that the force of his preaching lies in 'a demonstration of the Spirit's power', which some people take to mean miraculous healing. We don't always see that, though, when Paul's sharing his faith – more often than not, he relies on careful reasoning.

I think this is another aspect of the Spirit's power. God can give us the words and the arguments to use when we go out on a limb for Him – and often they seem to come from nowhere. Only recently, I got into a conversation with a random stranger and it ended up with us praying together on a street corner for God's help with some issues they were facing. I've also had conversations with serious academics who have seemed to find the simplicity of the cross and the grace of God hard to argue away. So, go for it, mate! Pray for the Spirit's power and get out there, even if it *is* in fear and trembling.

Prayer: I know I will never be the world's best speaker, but fill me with Your power and help me to share my faith effectively. Amen.

34/Mind matters

'But we have the mind of Christ.'
1 Corinthians 2:16b

What does this mean? Obviously, it can't mean
we know everything Jesus knows! To claim that
would be a bit bonkers, and probably heretical ...

There is, however, a profound truth here to get to
grips with. When you gave your life to Jesus, you
started a process of being made into His likeness.
Frankly, that's a long-term job for us all, and for
some of us – such as me – it feels like it's going to
take more than a lifetime! I don't know if you're
anything like me, but I've found that the more I
journey with Jesus in this life, and the closer I get
to God, the more I realise just how small I am and
just how big He is. I also find that the more I learn,
the more I appreciate that there's an awful lot I
don't know!

One thing I have discovered in particular is that
over the years my conscience gets sharper, too.
There are things in my life that bother me now

that never used to before, for example. And I think that's what it means to have the mind of Christ. He is chipping away at you, taking a rough block of granite and bit by bit shaping it into something awesome. I'm not yet at the finishing-cloth stage when it comes to the sculpting process, but, if I keep looking to Him, one day I will be.

So, take a moment today and use the prayer below to ask the Holy Spirit to keep fashioning you into the likeness of Jesus. Man up and give Him access to those dark places in your life you would rather that nobody saw. It's all part of the process.

Prayer: Lord, go over my life and chip away at those bits You don't like. Shape me into a man whose life pleases You. Amen.

35/ Peter

'Jesus replied, "Blessed are you, Simon son of Jonah ... I tell you that you are Peter, and on this rock I will build my church, and the gates of Hades will not overcome it. I will give you the keys of the kingdom of heaven; whatever you bind on earth will be bound in heaven, and whatever you loose on earth will be loosed in heaven."' `Matthew 16:17-19`

Peter is famous for three things: he walked on water (at least for a bit), he messed up massively and he was a key figure in the Early Church. He comes across in the Gospels as impetuous and up for a challenge, the sort of guy who wears his heart on his sleeve and leads from the front. Out of all the disciples, he was the one to say he was willing to die for Jesus (John 13:37).

Then the wheels came off.

In the dark hours that followed Jesus' execution, the disciples badly needed a leader. It could have been Peter's finest hour but instead it was a nightmare. Asked if he was a follower of Jesus (John 18), he had insisted he didn't even know Him and now he had to face up to the fact that, to save his own skin, he had turned his back on all he stood for: his Master, his mates and his moral courage.

That's a lot for a guy to deal with – but deal with it he does. Like many another man facing up to failure, he goes fishing. Seeing Jesus on the shoreline, he has a conversation with Him that turns him around and sets him back on track. Such was his transformation that later people would throw themselves into his shadow to get healed. History tells us that in the end he was crucified in Rome.

That's the difference between repenting and just feeling sorry for yourself. We all mess up. It's how we handle it that matters.

Prayer: When I've messed up, give me a heart like Peter's. Help me to steel myself to put things right. Amen.

36/Centurion

'For I myself am a man under authority, with soldiers under me. I tell this one, "Go," and he goes; and that one, "Come," and he comes. I say to my servant, "Do this," and he does it.' **Matthew 8:9**

A centurion in the Roman army had to be as hard as nails. In charge of 80 men (not 100 as you might think), he could have someone beaten and even executed for failing to follow orders. He would have been feared for his power but also respected because that power had been earned – he would have been a veteran of battle and commended by others. He had to be at least 30 years old and typically would have spent nearly half his life in the army by the time he got his command. This is the kind of guy Jesus was dealing with here.

It's important for us to realise, though, that while he might have seemed like a god to his men, he was also a man under authority himself. The very same punishments he could dish out could also be given to him. He was part of a chain of command.

That's why this exchange is so important for us to consider. This man, this commander of men, looked at Jesus and recognised that here he was dealing with a man of immense authority. He saw that He had a power way beyond his. After all, he knew that Jesus needed only to say the word and his servant would be healed. Amazing!

This guy was a man's man – not someone to have the wool pulled over his eyes. So, here's a question or three for you. Do you recognise the authority of Jesus in your life? Do you believe He is as powerful as the Bible says He is? And what difference would it make to you if you did?

Prayer: Give me this centurion's faith. Help me to live with a greater sense of Your power and authority in this world. Amen.

37/Nebuchadnezzar

'All this happened to King Nebuchadnezzar. Twelve months later, as the king was walking on the roof of the royal palace of Babylon, he said, "Is not this the great Babylon I have built as the royal residence, by my mighty power and for the glory of my majesty?"' **Daniel 4:28-30**

Nebuchadnezzar was born around 600 BC and was a man with huge power. He built Babylon up to be the largest city of its time – they reckon it covered nearly five square miles. He constructed one of the seven Ancient Wonders of the World, the 'hanging gardens' of Babylon, purely (it's said) so that his wife could be reminded of the mountains of her homeland. He was also a military commander and a political leader. No slouch, then.

His mistake was to attribute all his success to himself without honouring God, and to ignore the needs of the poor. He had been warned in a dream, which the prophet Daniel had interpreted for him, but hadn't taken any notice. It was to be his undoing – for a time.

Basically, until he acknowledged God, Nebuchadnezzar went mad and lived like a wild animal. It's said he ate grass like an ox and his hair grew like an eagle's feathers and his nails like the claws of a bird (Dan. 4:33). He lived like this for seven years. I suppose that's how long it took for him to sort himself out. Us blokes can be stubborn, I guess.

Perhaps it's a good thing for us to run a check on our pride levels from time to time. Do we pat ourselves on the back or do we attribute anything good we achieve to the One whose power works in and through us? Let's stay humble before God. It strikes me that He loves us too much *not* to discipline us. And when He does, we should welcome it, frankly – it's a sure way to get the rubbish in our lives sorted out!

Prayer: Keep me from making the same mistake as Nebuchadnezzar and being proud. Amen.

38/Achan

'But the Israelites were unfaithful in regard to the devoted things; Achan son of Karmi, the son of Zimri, the son of Zerah, of the tribe of Judah, took some of them. So the LORD's anger burned against Israel.' **Joshua 7:1**

This is a story of failure we would do very well to get hold of.

At the time when this incident took place, the armies of Israel were used to easy victories. Often, their enemies fled from them and they won the battle without losing a single man. However, Joshua 7 tells us how this all changed. The Israelites were routed and 36 of them were killed. Sure, they had 3,000 men, but still it came as a bit of a shock to an army that wasn't used to losing men, let alone battles.

So, why did it happen? Because someone had taken some plunder from an earlier battle, despite instructions not to do so because everything was 'devoted' to God (Josh. 6:18). The Israelites had been clearly warned that if anyone did take anything, they would put the whole camp at risk of destruction. Achan's flagrant disregard for God's instructions resulted in him and his entire family being put to death. That bit is hard for us to make sense of in our culture, but the lesson for us remains. One man's sin doesn't necessarily affect only him, it can also have an impact on his family and many others he has contact with.

I occasionally wonder why the Church sometimes seems so devoid of power. Perhaps there are issues of hidden sin that explain it. So, let's live clean for the sake of God's honour – and for the sake of our mates and our families, too.

Prayer: Help me to resist temptation and not fall into the trap of greed like Achan did. Amen.

39/Hosea

'When the LORD began to speak through Hosea, the LORD said to him, "Go, marry a promiscuous woman and have children with her, for like an adulterous wife this land is guilty of unfaithfulness to the LORD." So he married Gomer daughter of Diblaim, and she conceived and bore him a son.'

Hosea 1:2-3

When the Bible wants to talk about true love (as opposed to wishy-washy rom-com luuurve), it offers the example of Hosea. In a nutshell, God uses this guy to live out prophetically just how the people of Israel were treating Him. So, He gets Hosea to marry a loose woman called Gomer. She has three children, who are all given significant names – for example, the name of a place where many Israelites have died in battle and a name that means 'no pity', to show that God was going to wipe out the Northern Kingdom of Israel.

Not content with this, God then puts Hosea through a divorce (on the grounds that his wife keeps cheating on him) to show how unfaithful His people are being. Then He gets Hosea to forgive her and take her back, to show how He treats His people. What a nightmare! In fact, not only does Hosea take Gomer back, he also pays off all her debts because she has ended up in slavery! It's an astonishing read.

The story demonstrates two things. First, we learn just how much God loves us and is prepared to forgive us. Second, we see just how amazingly solid these Old Testament prophets really were. They were totally devoted to God. It's a real challenge to us, isn't it?

Prayer: I may not be a prophet, but show me Your heart for people and help me to live out my life in response to that. Help me to be faithful to You and others in my life. Amen.

[FIGHTING TALK]

40/Amazing grace

'... to the praise of his glorious grace, which he has freely given us in the One he loves.' **Ephesians 1:6**

John Newton wrote the hymn *Amazing Grace* back in the 1770s, but it has become so popular it is still often sung today:

Amazing grace! How sweet the sound
That saved a wretch like me!
I once was lost but now am found,
Was blind but now I see.

Jesus healed the blind, the sick and the lame and 'came to seek and to save the lost', and Newton describes God's free but undeserved gift of grace in terms of just such a miracle: 'I once was blind but now I see.' A.W. Tozer put it this way: 'The cross is the lightning rod of grace that short-circuits God's wrath to Christ so that only the light of His love remains for believers.'[1]

Through many dangers, toils and snares,
I have already come;
'Tis grace that brought me safe thus far,
And grace will lead me home.

Most Christians would agree that life as a believer in Jesus isn't easy – if life is ever easy! Newton sums up that sense in this verse. However, God gives us hope through His grace. If we accept Jesus into our lives, He will never leave us or forsake us, and His Spirit will guide us home!

Jesus paid the price we could never pay ourselves. Most guys like a bargain, and this gift was given to us for free. Isn't that worthy of praise? *Amazing* grace!

Prayer: Thank You, God, for Your amazing gift of grace, which has healed the divide between You and us. We don't deserve it, but You have given it to us freely. I ask for Your Holy Spirit to guide me on the narrow path that will take me home. Amen.

---

[1] http://crossquotes.org/category/a-w-tozer-quotes

41/Facing your giants 1

'A champion named Goliath, who was from Gath, came out of the Philistine camp. His height was over six cubits and a span.'
1 Samuel 17:4

Goliath was a nine-foot-tall, jeering, man-eating machine. He must have seemed invincible! The Israelite army ran from him in fear. Even their king, Saul, who was said to be among the tallest and bravest of them, was terrified of him.

David, a lowly shepherd whose eyes were fixed on God, indignantly asked the frightened soldiers around him: 'Who is this uncircumcised Philistine that he should defy the armies of the living God?' (1 Sam. 17:26). David felt insulted on God's account and this spurred him into action. His eagerness to take on Goliath, and his confidence that God would back him up, impressed the king. Saul even offered him his armour, but David said he'd rather stick with what he was used to. Armed with just five pebbles and a sling, he went out and, in God's strength, won the fight.

When we take our eyes off our circumstances and fix them on God, we realise that He is bigger than any enemy we may face, today or in the future. Giants such as our finances, our careers, our relationships, our addictions to money, sex or pornography - we can face them all when we go into battle with the Lord.

Prayer: Father, thank You that You are much bigger and more powerful than any giants I may face today. I pray that You will be with me in my battles with my Goliaths until, in Your strength, I conquer them. Amen.

42/Facing your giants 2

'If God is for us, who can be against us?' Romans 8:31b

As I suggested yesterday, our 'giants' can take many forms: money, relationships, sexual sin, low self-esteem, materialism, gluttony, pornography, health and fitness, career, cars or motorbikes – the list goes on almost forever. Maybe your particular giant is something you can control, maybe it's not – or maybe it's something you think you are in control of but actually it's in control of you!

You may have more than one giant heading your way; but God is on your side and He can bring you through anything if you allow Him to. He will walk with you through your rough patches, and if you can't walk He will carry you. God is our refuge and strength, an ever-present help in trouble (Psa. 46:1). He won't grow weary or faint – and He is willing and able to give you the strength to face and conquer your giants, whatever they are. You can't do it in your own strength, that's for sure!

When David killed Goliath, he drew on God's strength, not just his own. God helped him to win a battle that must have seemed impossible to everyone else – 'impossible' is not in His dictionary! The Bible says that 'God is faithful; he will not let you be tempted beyond what you can bear. But when you are tempted, he will also provide a way out so that you can endure it' (1 Cor. 10:13). So, join David today, whatever you're going through, and draw on God's strength. He has a purpose and a plan for your life and He will guide you into it.

Prayer: Father, You are the Pioneer and Perfecter of my faith. Keep my eyes fixed on You. Renew my faith in You so that I can learn to stand in Your strength to face and conquer my giants. Amen.

43/Stand your ground!

'Therefore put on the full armour of God, so that when the day of evil comes, you may be able to stand your ground, and after you have done everything, to stand.'
Ephesians 6:13

Every day, we go into battle, both in our heads and in the world. The apostle Paul says that our fight is not against other people but against the spiritual forces of evil. As believers, we need to strive to be the men God intends us to be and stand our ground against Satan and his wiles. To do that, we need to put on the full armour of God, which Paul itemises for us:

• The belt of truth. Lying is one of men's biggest weaknesses – we think that if we brush things under the carpet, everything will be OK, but they always bite us on the backside. Tell the truth!

• The breastplate of righteousness, which protects our vital organs from damage. You can't survive without your vital organs, so act righteously!

- The boots that are 'the readiness that comes from the gospel of peace'. If the gospel makes you eager to get out there as a peacekeeper, you'll find that the stones and thorns underfoot don't bother you.
- The shield of faith. A strong faith in God will give us the protection we need to win the battle with the forces of evil in today's world.
- The helmet of salvation. Remember that Jesus has defeated death and Satan on the cross. We have the victory through His shed blood.
- The sword of the Spirit, which is the Word of God. This is the only weapon in the armour of God, but it can stop Satan in his tracks. Jesus Himself used scripture when He was being tempted.

Prayer: Father, help me to recognise Satan's wiles and stand my ground against him. Remind me daily that I need to put on Your armour and use it in the fight. Thank You that I can share in Jesus' victory over Satan on the cross. Amen.

44/Power

> '... our gospel came to you not simply with words but also with power, with the Holy Spirit and deep conviction. You know how we lived among you for your sake.'
> **1 Thessalonians 1:5**

When we speak up for Jesus, we are engaging in a spiritual exercise. We aren't just uttering words, we are declaring a cosmic-scale truth. Whenever people in the Bible proclaimed Jesus, it was followed by what we call 'signs and wonders' – the deaf got their hearing back, the blind got their sight back and the lame started to walk again. The miracles were a signpost to God's kingdom, as well as tangible proof that He cares about people. Does this mean that every time we speak about Jesus ourselves, people get healed? I don't believe so; but I do think we need to work on our levels of faith, hope and expectation.

I also love the way Paul says he spoke with deep conviction. You can imagine it, can't you? Total belief and confidence in the power of Jesus and the truth of His message. I can see Paul refusing to yield ground in the face of the most strident opponent – he was probably the equivalent of Chuck Norris when it comes to preaching and speaking about Jesus!

So, let's up our confidence levels and start to believe we will see the power of God break through when we speak up about Jesus. Let's have solid conviction that we speak the truth and do so with power and the Holy Spirit. You may ask how we get to that point. Well, as with all things in this game, it's not rocket science. We need to spend time with God, read His word – use *The Manual*, of course! – and actually put into practice what we read. Let's go for it!

Prayer: May I see the power of the Holy Spirit at work as I step up and step out to proclaim Your gospel. Amen.

45/Copy cat

'You became imitators of us and of the Lord, for you welcomed the message in the midst of severe suffering with the joy given by the Holy Spirit.' **1 Thessalonians 1:6**

The church in Thessalonica went on to become a model for believers in Macedonia and Achaia (modern-day Greece, more or less). That fact makes this verse even more hard-hitting, because the Christians there achieved that status by imitating Paul and his team in their imitation of the Lord. In other words, the DNA of their faith was first-class. What you are formed by, you become.

So, what about us? What are we modelling? How are we leading our lives in front of those who are new followers of Jesus – and those who have yet to cross the starting line? It's a massive challenge to us. Our conduct could be responsible for people really going for it – or just hanging back. I firmly believe that we control the culture of the environments in which we live and work, for example. If we drink too much, we 'give permission' to others to do the same. The sort of humour we go in for can set the tone in the office or the pub. How generous (or otherwise) we are will have a profound effect on those around us.

New believers, in particular, need role models to look up to and take their lead from. It's a fact that they will be looking up to you, whether you like it or not. The best way forward is for each of us to be discipling someone and moving them closer to Christ. So, take a good look at your life and ask yourself: What would I pick up from someone living like that, if I was just an observer looking on?

Prayer: Help me to be an effective role model whose life sets a good example of how to follow Jesus. Amen.

46/Idols

'The Lord's message rang out from you not only in Macedonia and Achaia – your faith in God has become known everywhere. Therefore we do not need to say anything about it, for they themselves report what kind of reception you gave us. They tell how you turned to God from idols to serve the living and true God.'

1 Thessalonians 1:8-9

So, the Thessalonian effect continues! Not only are these Christians out there 'bumping their gums' about Jesus but they're living it as well. Paul knows this because word is getting back to him from third parties that these people's lives are different. From being full-on idolators, they now worship only Jesus. It's obviously such a radical about-turn that it is massively newsworthy. Think about it: this news is travelling huge distances by word of mouth only – it's not as if they could get on Facebook about it! In other words, this is compelling stuff.

It leads me to think about the distinctiveness of my own life as a bloke. What differences do people see in me that make them sit up and take notice? Here are the thoughts that come to my mind as I ponder on what it might mean to live counter to our culture: Am I known for generosity in a materialistic world? Do I have idols? Am I characterised by joy rather than complaint? In the face of celebrity culture, am I practising humility and grace?

In other words, am I distinctly different to the point where people talk about it? I don't know about you, but for my own part there's work to do!

Prayer: I want to be distinctly different for the King of kings. Help me to make right choices that go against the flow of our culture. Amen.

47/Plain truth

'And to wait for his Son from heaven, whom he raised from the dead – Jesus, who rescues us from the coming wrath.' **1 Thessalonians 1:10**

With so much Christian material out there on how to be a better person – in other words, Christian life-coaching – it's good to remind ourselves of some good ol' gospel facts. Jesus didn't come to this planet just to make us better people, He came here to redeem us. If it wasn't for Him, we'd be facing hell – something we barely mention any more in our churches. I used to have a Bible called the *Good News Bible*, but the truth is that it contains bad news as well. It may be unpalatable but that doesn't mean it isn't true.

The bottom line is that we need to remember more often that a man died for us.

A couple of years back, I and a few friends wrote a discipleship tool for blokes called *the Code*. Basically, it's 12 statements of intent for men who follow Jesus to live their lives by – a kind of Christ-centred honour code. It starts by saying that He is our Captain, Brother, Rescuer and Friend. (I like it that we say 'rescuer' – we don't remember that part of the gospel enough!) One of my friends wrote a prayer in response. It's a bit longer than is normal for *The Manual* but here it is anyway. I think it sums things up brilliantly.

Prayer: You are my Maker. I am Your work in progress.
You are my Redeemer. You paid the price for putting me right and forgiving me, with Your life. All I can do is thank You and say that I owe You everything.
You are my Rescuer. I have been salvaged.
You are my Owner. I am Your slave.
You are my Friend. We are friends.
You are my Commander. I am Your warrior.
You are my Brother. We are brothers.
You are my Father.
I am Your son.
Amen.

48/Crack on regardless...

'You know, brothers and sisters, that our visit to you was not without results. We had previously suffered and been treated outrageously in Philippi, as you know, but with the help of our God we dared to tell you his gospel in the face of strong opposition.' **1 Thessalonians 2:1-2**

Paul faced massive opposition wherever he went. I'm not just talking about people being upset with him, either. He was flogged, thrown into jail (which would have been more like a dungeon than any prison today) and in constant danger of losing his head – literally. Despite this, however, he cracked on with the job, always ready to give an account of his faith and take the hit that inevitably followed. We, on the other hand, can often be too scared to share our faith in a coffee shop or staffroom!

I wonder where this fear comes from? Perhaps it's something to do with maintaining our coolness, in the odd belief that people will think worse of us for 'admitting' we follow Jesus. Perhaps it's a fear of rejection? Or a simple matter of not knowing what to say? A good place to start when sharing your faith is just to tell people your story. A friend of mine gave me a great tip. He said he starts by asking the other person if they've ever had a 'spiritual experience'. Most people have, and that then gives him an excuse to share his story. It has led to some amazing conversations.

So, stuff your nerves, or whatever it is that stops you. We're in the business of facing up to opposition – and those who follow Jesus attract it because we have an enemy who wants to silence us! Perhaps you could start by recalling how you first met Jesus. Write it down – and then just make sure you tell someone about it.

_____

Prayer: Help me to face up to opposition – including my fears – when it comes to sharing my faith. Give me a chance today to tell someone about the hope I have and how I came by it. Amen.

_____

49/People pleaser

'For the appeal we make does not spring from error or impure motives, nor are we trying to trick you. On the contrary, we speak as those approved by God to be entrusted with the gospel. We are not trying to please people but God, who tests our hearts.'
1 Thessalonians 2:3-4

For a number of years, I worked as a salesman. Mostly I worked in the financial services sector, but when I was at school I had a part-time job selling furniture. It was much the same, really. You identified the benefits of the product that matched your prospective client's needs and you pitched accordingly. You avoided any bad-news angles and made everything sound easy, like this product was the best thing ever. I was quite successful at it.

I see the same thing happening when people pitch the gospel. They find an angle that meets someone's emotional and spiritual needs and try to close the deal on that basis. The problem with this is that it very rarely leads to repentance, if ever. Here, Paul insists that he isn't trying to trick anyone and doesn't have impure motives. What he means is that he isn't a people pleaser.

It's worth bearing this in mind. I've found it an uncomfortable fact that when I communicate the gospel I have to go through the pain barrier and accept that I'm going to offend some people. The truth is, though, that we live out our lives to an audience of one and it's God we should be seeking to please in all we say and do. And if the things that please God offend some people, we just have to take that on the chin. So, let's speak and act as men approved by God. Seek to honour Him and the rest will follow. Be a people pleaser and, I can assure you, you will never be truly content.

Prayer: Let me speak as someone approved by God, a man who can be trusted with the gospel. Make my focus be on pleasing God and not men. Amen.

50/Mateship

'But, brothers and sisters, when we were orphaned by being separated from you for a short time (in person, not in thought), out of our intense longing we made every effort to see you.' **1 Thessalonians 2:17**

Being a fairly typical bloke, I guess I'm not that good at keeping up with friends. I tend to bond with people wherever I am and then, when I move off, it's back to square one. It's not that I'm callous, that I don't care about people or pray for them; it's just that my attention tends to be focused on whatever I'm doing at the time and I don't often feel separation keenly. My wife is completely different. She can be on the phone to someone in the morning for ages and then meet up with them to go shopping in the afternoon – I always wonder what on earth they find to talk about. If I talk to a friend on the phone for ten minutes, I think that's enough for six months!

Paul bares his heart here and it's clear that, when it comes to relationships, he rocks to a different tune. He feels the pain of being apart from the church physically, to the point where he describes it as being orphaned! I wonder what that says to us about the way we give ourselves to friendships in the church. Do we give all of ourselves emotionally? Do we take time to connect with other blokes? Do we share life's ups and downs? Are we there for each other? The reason I ask is that it seems to me it's only in sharing the joy and pain together that we create a strong sense of brotherhood.

Personally, I think that every man who follows Jesus should be walking in the company of at least three other men. If you're not doing this, have a serious think about building it into your life.

Prayer: I intend to be a man who journeys with other men wholeheartedly. Make me a solid and dependable mate. Amen.

51/Enemy action

'For we wanted to come to you – certainly I, Paul, did, again and again – but Satan blocked our way.'
1 Thessalonians 2:18

Bad stuff happens. Sometimes, even the best-laid plans go pear-shaped. That's just life!

However, there is another dimension to this for us as followers of Jesus. We believe we are engaged in spiritual warfare – we may not always be aware of the battle that rages around us but it's happening. We have an enemy who seeks to frustrate us at every turn and sometimes he succeeds. Now, of course we don't want to be seeing Satan in everything – that's why I began this by saying that sometimes it's just life. However, we do need to keep our spiritual eyes and ears open.

I recently applied for a visa to a country I'd visited many times before. I was going to meet old friends and make new ones and investigate possible mission work in the future. I've never had a problem getting a visa before, but twice I was refused – which was tricky because I was due to fly on 2 January and it was now 20 December. I duly filled out all the forms a third time, but this time I rallied people to pray. I had a deep sense that Satan didn't want me to visit this country. The last time my family was there, my daughter had broken her arm and while she was in casualty an armed gang had stormed in and shot someone in front of her! Sometimes you really do think your work is upsetting the devil …

On this occasion, however, he didn't win. My visa arrived two days before Christmas. It was a remarkable turnaround I put down to my efficient admin and a miracle brought about by prayer. The bottom line is this: We will face opposition – that's the spiritual life – but fight back with prayer and never quit!

Prayer: Help me to spot the enemy's attacks when they come. Prompt me to pray when I need to and help me to fight through, no matter how tough it gets. Amen.

52/Reinforcements

> 'We sent Timothy, who is our brother and co-worker in God's service in spreading the gospel of Christ, to strengthen and encourage you in your faith, so that no one would be unsettled by these trials. For you know quite well that we are destined for them.' **1 Thessalonians 3:2-3**

The movie men seem to be obsessed with films about the solo superwarrior type of guy. You know the sort: he's a one-man army who can skydive, fly helicopters, drive tanks and defeat whole battalions single-handed and yet still knows how to prepare oysters and is great with kids. He's the do-it-all king. If anyone does pitch up to give him a helping hand, it's usually just so that he can show how weak and unmanly they are. It's totally ridiculous, of course – no man is all-sufficient or omni-competent.

I don't believe we were made to be solo superwarriors, I think we were made to work in teams and journey with a sense of brotherhood and belonging. That's why Paul dispatching Timothy to the Thessalonians was so important. They needed input from outside to strengthen and encourage them. I wonder what you're like at accepting a helping hand or having some blokes get alongside you. Are you the type of fella who likes to go it alone or are you open to having people speaking into your life and bringing words of encouragement? It's a funny thing, really, but so many of us men find it hard to receive from people – we think it's a sign of weakness.

Personally, I'll take all the help and encouragement I can get. After all, you know that at some point someone will come along and say or do something to discourage you! So, listen, take all the help you can get. Accept encouragement and draw strength from your mates. Don't try to be a one-man army, be part of a brotherhood!

Prayer: Give me an open heart and help me to accept encouragement and draw strength from others. Amen.

53/Compromise

'For this reason, when I could stand it no longer, I sent to find out about your faith. I was afraid that in some way the tempter had tempted you and that our labours might have been in vain.' **1 Thessalonians 3:5**

One of Paul's biggest concerns, it often seems, was the preservation of truth against the background of an Empire that was big on what we call 'syncretism'. The Romans used a method of control that basically went like this: 'You can keep your religion, your language, your customs – as long as you embrace those of Rome as well'. It was a brilliant strategy. As long as people worshipped Rome's gods – and especially the Emperor – alongside their own, they'd be left alone. Almost everyone across the Empire went along with this – but not the followers of Jesus. In general, they stood firm and refused to accept this compromise. That's one reason why so many ended up in the Colosseum or being burnt as human torches in Nero's garden.

We need to ask ourselves where the temptations to adulterate our faith are in our culture. Perhaps it's stuff to do with possessions – this is a consumption-driven culture, after all. Perhaps it's the idols of health and appearance? I've noticed how sales of 'Be a better you' kind of books seem to outstrip by far those of books that encourage us to respond to God's heart for the poor.

Perhaps a good exercise is to make a list of the things that motivate you in life and compare them with the things Jesus wants us to be motivated by. That's not to say, of course, that all ambition and all striving for money are wrong. What is wrong potentially is the things in the background that drive you forward. I know someone who is brilliant at making money but gives most of it away. 'I think God likes to keep us lean,' he told me once. Challenging stuff.

Prayer: Keep me from compromise. Help me to stay sharp on the things that are important to You. Amen.

54/Luuurve

'May the Lord make your love increase and overflow for each other and for everyone else, just as ours does for you.' **1 Thessalonians 3:12**

It's hard to know how to deal with a verse like this when you're writing a devotional for blokes. I mean, this isn't exactly a rom-com, or the book equivalent of those puppy-dog posters you see in churches up and down the country. It's meant to be full-on, straight-to-the-point stuff for fellas! So, what on earth do we take from this?

Well, let's nail one myth that often floats around men's work. Just because we say that some stuff in church is really girlie doesn't mean we are anti emotion. Nor are we anti blokes giving each other a hug or a slap on the back. We're certainly not anti forming deep bonds of friendship to the point where you can tell someone you love them as a brother. There's nothing wrong with that at all. And before you worry that I'm going soft, I still ban blokes waving streamers around at our conferences. Tears, yes. Streamers, no.

I do think us men need to cultivate bonds of friendship that go really deep. Friendships that are founded on sharing the ups and downs, the heartaches, struggles and stresses. I think that what Paul says here would make a very challenging prayer for the average bloke like you or me – that we would not merely love others more but overflow with love for everyone. What would us men look like if we were characterised by love? World-changing, perhaps?

Prayer: Let me overflow with love not only for my family and my mates but for everyone I have contact with. May I be known as a man of love, with compassion for everyone – even people I wouldn't naturally get along with. Amen.

55/Strengthen me

> 'May he strengthen your hearts so that you will be blameless and holy in the presence of our God and Father when our Lord Jesus comes with all his holy ones.'
>
> **1 Thessalonians 3:13**

Note what Paul says here. He prays that God will strengthen our hearts, but he doesn't mean physically. The Bible often talks about the heart, and I've written earlier in this series about Proverbs 4:23, which tells us to, 'above all else, guard your heart, for everything you do flows from it.'

So, let's think, as we finish our short blast through the opening chapters of 1 Thessalonians, what it takes to make our hearts strong. We know that physical exercise has huge benefits for a long life and general well-being, but what about our spiritual dimension? First, we need to make sure we spend time in God's Word. That's the primary thing, because it's from the Bible that we learn how to live in a way that pleases God.

Then, we need to do things that challenge our hearts. That means we need to live with a 'counter' spirit. When we are wronged, we should love back. When someone speaks ill of us, we should shrug it off (Proverbs 12:16 says: 'Fools show their annoyance at once, but the prudent overlook an insult'). We should seek justice and practise compassion and generosity in word and deed. We should devote ourselves to prayer – sometimes in a season of prayer that's more intense. We should practise forgiveness – you know you're on the money with forgiveness when it hurts! We should learn to be meek and behave humbly, to open our lives and our homes. I could go on. These sort of things will strengthen our hearts like a daily 20 minutes on a rowing machine!

So, go for it – and remember to embrace the idea of a counter spirit. It's when you do the opposite of what the world would do!

Prayer: Strengthen my resolve to strengthen my heart. Help me to live with a spirit that goes counter to the spirit of the world. Amen.

56/The battle begins

> 'Then Jesus was led by the Spirit into the wilderness to be tempted by the devil.' **Matthew 4:1**

I've always found this rather fascinating. It's not like the devil is ambushing Jesus here – He is actually led into the wilderness deliberately so that a battle can take place.

I believe that sometimes God does the same to us. In order to strengthen us and refine us, He leads us into situations that will test our mettle. Sometimes, too, He may lead us into situations in which we can weaken the power of the enemy in our lives. When we stand our ground against Satan, he does tend to back off in the end.

What he does do, however, is target our vulnerabilities. That's why it's so important to be wearing the armour of God as we journey (see Day 43). We need to be ready for battle at all times, not least because Satan doesn't believe in a fair fight! He uses guerrilla warfare tactics against us – metaphorically speaking, he sneaks up behind us and shoots us in the back, then runs away before we even see him coming.

So, stay alert and ready for the challenge. At some point, the enemy is bound to attack you. At some point, God may well commit you to a battle. You should be ready for both eventualities by staying armoured up.

Prayer: Strengthen me and ready me for the battles that lie ahead. When You put me to the test or send me into single combat against the enemy, please be with me. Amen.

57/Fightback

'After fasting for forty days and forty nights, he was hungry. The tempter came to him and said, "If you are the Son of God, tell these stones to become bread." Jesus answered, "It is written: 'Man shall not live on bread alone, but on every word that comes from the mouth of God.'"'
Matthew 4:2-4

Here's an object lesson in how to fight Satan. Typically, the enemy goes for a weak spot. No honour here – it's like a boxer constantly going for his opponent's cut eye. Jesus hasn't eaten for 40 days – to say He is hungry is a bit of an understatement!

So, how does He fight back? Simples: He uses the sword of the Spirit, the very words of God. Evidently it works, because the devil doesn't linger on the point – he knows it is a lost cause. And so he simply ups the stakes, as we will see when we look at the next exchange of blows in this fight.

The stuff to take away from this opening round is this: the devil doesn't go in for a warm-up, he piles straight in with a low blow to the gut. He gets his punch in quick and it goes in hard. We fight back by being close to God and His Word. Simply gritting your teeth is not enough when it comes to spiritual warfare. Nor is just praying more loudly or looking all spiritually intense. You need to be grounded in the truth if you're going to fight effectively against the devil. If that's not an incentive to remain in God's Word, I don't know what is. Us guys have got to be ready for the scrap when it comes.

Prayer: Help me to be ready for a scrap with the devil – and help me to stand up to the low blows when they come. Amen.

58/Power hour

'Then the devil took him to the holy city and set him on the highest point of the temple. "If you are the Son of God," he said, "throw yourself down. For it is written: 'He will command his angels concerning you, and they will lift you up in their hands, so that you will not strike your foot against a stone.'" Jesus answered him, "It is also written: 'Do not put the Lord your God to the test.'"' **Matthew 4:5-7**

Some say that men's weaknesses can be boiled down to three Gs: gold, girls and glory. Or, to put it another way, money, sex and power. Satan failed to tempt Jesus with His basic human need of food, so now he appeals to His ego. What he's saying is this: 'You say You're the Son of God but I don't believe you. Prove it! If You're so precious to God, He won't let any harm come to You.'

I've felt the challenge of that 'Prove it!' myself, many times. It can really reel you in if you're not careful. There's a very basic need in men to be seen to be all we say we are and more, but to respond to that challenge is pretty childish, really. If we're secure as blokes and truly know who and what we are in Christ, we have no need to go around trying to prove it.

So, next time you feel this pressure on you to be 'the big man' and show everyone how special you are, just get a grip and crack on, confident that God knows who you are and what does it matter anyway what other people think?

Prayer: Let me be secure, not insecure. Help me to rise above it if people show how little they think of me. Help me to focus instead on what You think of me. Amen.

59/ Power play

'Again, the devil took him to a very high mountain and showed him all the kingdoms of the world and their splendour.' **Matthew 4:8**

Men have always lusted after power. The need for it can drive them to the edge – it's even been known to drive them mad. I remember once listening to a very senior politician talk about it. He said that there comes a time when you need to walk away from high office because otherwise you can lose all sense of reality. He recalled how he suddenly had to send his own emails and drive his own car and said that it felt like starting all over again. Not having an entourage around him left him feeling exposed and vulnerable. In other words, he had forgotten what it was like to live a normal life.

Nonetheless, despite the obvious pitfalls, it is still an attractive proposition to many men to have absolute power. So, Satan tempts Jesus with it. The intriguing thing here, of course, is that Jesus has already rejected such power by becoming a man like you and me. He was with God in the beginning and He has the name to which one day every knee will bow. He holds the keys to the grave and will one day consign the devil permanently to hell. Yet He is still tempted here to have absolute worldly power given to Him. Had He succumbed, it would have derailed his mission completely. The stakes are incredibly high and so the temptation to say 'yes' must be very strong.

The answer Jesus gives says it all. In order to keep things in perspective ourselves, we must remember that, whoever we are, we are servants of the Living God. Ultimately, we worship and serve Him only. That's worth bearing in mind.

Prayer: I worship and serve You alone, God. Protect me from lust for power and help me to keep in perspective what it's really all about. Amen.

60/Be the light

'Live as children of light.' **Ephesians 5:8**

Let's close out Book 5 with something I wrote a few days before the end of 2012. It's not a poem, it's a statement. I hope it challenges you.

Be the Light

Be known in this life for the way you give,
   not the way you take.
Live generously in word and deed.
If you lend anything, do it as if you will never
   get back what you lent.
Travel lightly through life, holding nothing
   material too tightly.
Only hold tight your family, the people you
   call 'friend', your faith in God.
Be known for being a man of justice, not
   blind to the needs of the world.
Be compassionate.
Be kind to your fellow man, make mercy and
   justice your travelling companions.
Seek to do what is good, resist evil, never
   allow hatred of men a root in your life.

Only hate and despise that which imprisons
men's hearts
And takes them on a road to hell.
Love your family and treasure moments,
enjoy friendships.
Spend more time with people.
Always give people the benefit of the doubt
and believe the best.
Be prepared to get hurt, walk humbly,
live vulnerably.
Guard your heart, keep it soft and never let it
harden or your enemy wins.
Work hard but don't make work your master.
Leader or follower, you are a servant.
Whatever you do, you do before an audience
of one.
Be diligent, honest, respectful and known as
a man who finishes the task.
Take criticism well, listen and take advice
or you'll fall into error.
You'll one day breathe your last breath –
Live life in readiness for the final journey.
Keep God close, walk in repentance before Him.
Make sure you are at peace with all men.
Point others to the place where you are heading.
When that time comes, if your heart is right and
you are walking with the King,
You will receive a faith hero's welcome.

THE MANUAL

More Bible notes for men written by Carl Beech.

Contain:

- 60 daily readings and prayers
- Two guest contributions
- Themes to encourage and challenge you

The Manual – Book 1:
Power/Poker/Pleasure/Pork Pies
ISBN: 978-1-85345-769-2

The Manual – Book 2:
Fighters/Keepers/Losers/Reapers
ISBN: 978-1-85345-770-8

The Manual – Book 3:
Son/See/Surf
ISBN: 978-1-85345-883-5

The Manual – Book 4:
Attitude/Gratitude/Proper Food
ISBN: 978-1-85345-886-6

The Manual – Book 6:
Sowing/Growing/Knowing
ISBN: 978-1-85345-944-3

Also available in ebook formats

Courses and seminars

Publishing and new media

Conference facilities

Transforming lives

CWR's vision is to enable people to experience personal transformation through applying God's Word to their lives and relationships.

Our Bible-based training and resources help people around the world to:
• Grow in their walk with God
• Understand and apply Scripture to their lives
• Resource themselves and their church
• Develop pastoral care and counselling skills
• Train for leadership
• Strengthen relationships, marriage and family life and much more.

CWR Applying God's Word
to everyday life and relationships

CWR, Waverley Abbey House,
Waverley Lane, Farnham,
Surrey GU9 8EP, UK

Telephone: **+44 (0)1252 784700**
Email: **info@cwr.org.uk**
Website: **www.cwr.org.uk**

Registered Charity No 294387
Company Registration No 1990308

Our insightful writers provide daily Bible-reading notes and other resources for all ages, and our experienced course designers and presenters have gained an international reputation for excellence and effectiveness.

CWR's Training and Conference Centre in Surrey, England, provides excellent facilities in an idyllic setting – ideal for both learning and spiritual refreshment.

it's time for a new kind of man

connecting
men to Jesus
& the church to men

Partner with us
Connect a men's group
Start a men's group
Join a movement

Equipping and resourcing you to
share Jesus with the men around you

networking || events   resources || training

cvm.org.uk

CVM is a movement that offers a range of advice,
resources and men's events across the UK and be
The Hub, Unit 2, Dunston Rd, Chesterfield S41 8XA Tel: 01246 4
Registered Charity in England & Wales (No. 1071663)
A Company Ltd by Guarantee (No. 3623498)